In the Meat Years

In the Meat Years

Poems by

Kindra M. McDonald

Kelsay Books

Cover art by Lily Sun
Cover layout by Shay Culligan

ISBN: 978-1-950462-14-8

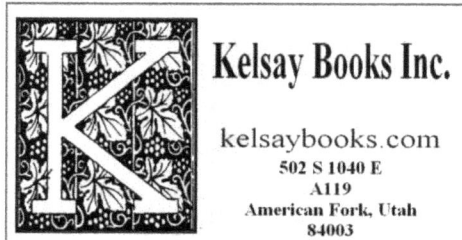

Kelsay Books Inc.

kelsaybooks.com
502 S 1040 E
A119
American Fork, Utah
84003

For my mom and my mother-in-law, Shirley and Maria,
thank you for your incredible strength
and showing me the best ways to nourish others.

For Adam, for feeding my spirit, for being the bloom in drought.

Then winter came and there was little left between us
skin and bones of love won't make a meal.
—Josh Ritter

Acknowledgments

Thank you to the presses in which the following work has previously appeared:

The Watershed Review: "Avgolemono", "ripe", and "Visitation"
The Nearest Poem Anthology: "Setting the Table"
Barely South Review: "Honeysuckle"
From the Depths - Haunted Waters Press Poetry Open finalist: "Hope Without Light" and "What do I Know of Loss?"
Bird's Thumb: "Recoil"
From the Chapbook, Elements & Briars (Red Bird Chapbooks): "Primroses" – (Formerly "Yawning")
Likely Red Press: "Crossing"
From the Chapbook, Concealed Weapons (ELJ Publications): "Cherries"
The Tishman Review: "On the day she decides to leave"
SWWIM: "Drowning"
Porkbelly Press: "Carnivore"
Poetry Society of Virginia - 2019 Contest Winners: "Brood" and "What do you See?"

Thank you for holding this book in your hands,
for loving words and for supporting small presses.

Contents

Avgolemono

February, Ohio:
In an eternal depth
of seasonal depression, foggy
headed and sleepsick, mother
would rally
some Sunday mornings
to make soup for us.
The Greek egg and lemon soup
from her newlywed years when
as a 19-year-old with a toddler
and a stomach full, a new child soon,
her neighbor who spoke very little
English, (other than the common
tongue of weary mothers), taught
her in a cramped kitchen the comfort
food of her family. All day the chicken
would boil, warming the house; the eggs
were broken one by one and beaten, sweet
discs of lemony sunlight cut and squeezed
into the mix. Even August sun was not that bright.
Slowly, the hot broth was stirred ladle by ladle
into the eggs. This was the careful part. She'd scoop
dry orzo into a margarine container—
an instant maraca for the baby, a distraction
while the broth and eggs slowly married but never curdled.
The fog in the house would lift, the broth become opaque
and thick. The day felt longer, the night shorter, the cold
tolerable. Then it was possible to hear a songbird returning home.

Setting the Table

When I was young I used to imagine
that Forks were men and Spoons were women.
The Forks would prey on the Spoons
and their sleek, smooth, slightly arched
backs if it weren't for the gallant Knives
that protected the small curve of Spoon's head
on the soft white cotton napkins.

The Knives were long and straight-backed,
gentle and strong, with teeth that warned
the Fork, whose tines rose like claws,
to keep his mouth shut.

My father was both Fork and Knife.
Sometimes he could rise up like the tilted
head of a Fork and with eyes as bright
as silver pierce me in triplicate.
Other times he was like a Knife, standing tall
warding off enemies—those that break the plates,
and protecting me like a straight-backed soldier,
gently tucking in the white cotton sheets of my bed.

Scooping up soup, I wondered how she could live
with her bent head. Could Spoon learn to meld,
to mold, to change into other forms?
Things not so easily bent, broken and used
to scrape out what is thrown away.

Daffodils

He was born in the month of daffodils
after years of miscarriage, after all those girls
and giving up, and trying again, after the stewing
of summer, the silences, the awful thrumming of
the moth furious at the porch light late nights
the cold winter quickening the revival
when the green tips point out of still cold soil
and yellow cups are lining sidewalks, it is in this
promise of hope, of warmth to come that I remember
his birthday every year, celebrate your boy
with a vase of sun.

You Eat Like a Bird

No one has said to me.
When I was growing curves
my mom was diminishing hers
with months of Slim-Fast shakes
and melba toast, cottage cheese
and Virginia Slims
weigh-ins coincided
with back to school shopping
where I would try
to button new stiff jeans
around my growing waist
hate every hot dressing room
every three-way mirror.
If I could fall asleep
with my stomach growling
I would smile,
wish my hip bones thin
as threads
work my thigh
master into submission
make myself take up
as little room as possible.

I would eat two grains
of raw wild rice, drink cup
after cup of water, believed
I could feel the swell of the specks
in my stomach filling me full
to bursting. At my sister's
wedding she grows faint
with hunger, glows in her
wedding gown, a wisp

of a bride. We throw
rice as they run hand
in hand to their future
a toss for fertility, for growing
breasts and belly, for birthing
hips and a softer face—
all those grains for the birds
on the ground. I save two
in my palm to place under
my tongue when the growling
keeps me awake.

Depression Dialogue

You've become birdlike. Tufts poking up
from your shorn hair, ends soft and spindly
eyes cast up looking for any nest which might
take you. Like a starling taught to recite lines,
sit on the edge of a stage, and call up to the actors
from the invisible verge, you cling.

> *They come at me in the dark poking at my*
> *eyes. Pray this goes away, their sharp beaks of accusation*
> *carrion circle above, shrieks as dark as smoke*

I would build a nest of love, pull twigs from concern,
pinecones out of worry,
dirt from the earth, to cradle your chest
roost with arms wrapped tight around this mess.

> *It is torture to wonder what keeps them aloft*
> *how do they learn to balance?*
> *Coasting on a cloud carrying such heaviness*
> *on their so small wings how they surface such*
> *secrecy deep from the ruffled feathers of our dark*

You are a stranger now—
hard where you used to be soft
all ribcage and cartilage, all
tendon and bone, all blank-eyed
wet face. Do birds feel the
loss of molting? This little bit of down
shed and stolen from them for dusters.
How attached were they to this weight whose loss
leaves them flightless and weak, drunk on their feet.

Mouth full of bones that click
against my canines
clatter like Scrabble tiles
grinding tufts of feathered fluff
down my throat gagging on the not yet
claws of tiny feet pointing inside out

Feathers fall from your battered pillow
that knows so well the curve of your head.
Steal them for a hat, lure a trout to
surface, make an arrow fly true,
thank the bird that donated it
for flying by and setting a course to follow home.

It is the season of baby birds readying to hatch in warm
nests. I see them now limp in the mouth of the neighbor's
dog mother squawking to the empty sky, feathers sunk in
summer mud

Wisteria

Each April as it climbs over interstate barriers
and hangs itself over guardrails it shows up
before the leaves have quite filled in the bare
branches. I know it's the anniversary of the finishing

line bombs, when I stared stunned at the news where friends
had trained for months to run those Boston hills, forced
myself outside to breathe and saw the climbing vines.
The wisteria, in their small window of life, was in full bloom.

Fat, grape clumps where there had been nothing. Clinging
to the phone poles, on sides of highway trees, on broken
sheds, over rusted cars. Each spring it's a surprise to see where
they will flourish, how they thrive, how now they are a promise.

Choices

Today I walk into a wedding
in the gardens, the bride brilliant

white, glowing against so much green
the groom in charcoal, the bark of an ash branch

the willows are curtains waving between them
1st Corinthians echoes over the last breath of daffodils

the new blooms of azaleas, the bright bursts of color
here now and gone next week. All of the paths

are marked with benches, all the benches marked with
plaques in memory of someone who loved this place

like I do, protective of my spot under the dogwood,
our state tree, whose flowering marks our first kiss

shaded and hidden just out of view, I watch the
exchange of vows and rings, the kiss and applause

that moves across the water like tadpole ripples.
The long-necked turtle surfaces and disappears

and the toddlers do not make safe choices as they wander
near the bank to grasp at clover and snowbells.

I find a red leather glove that had grown warm
in the sun, just last week it swept snow from this seat.

The crape myrtles planted in a row link their lower limbs
like legs of dancers in a kick line

and just this hour has made me
think I can wake up tomorrow.

Bend

The morning
after tornadoes
tore through
town took
down a church
bricks flown
sticks stuck
clean through
wooden pews
the tulips
that had been
so straight and
tightly closed
flipped over
the rim of their
glass vase—bent
towards the sun
tilted their cups
up black stars
shining out
sassing storm
clouds to keep
moving south
reminding me
the devil finds
our weakness
when we don't

The Cruelest Month

She said her headaches we'd been worrying about were a brain
tumor, then bent over laughing at her April fool's prank.

Lincoln and Jesus both died on Good Friday, this year
Easter is a joke.

My sister celebrates her birthday, which is also my father-in-law's
birthday. But this year, and every year from now on, I will only
think about the last thing I said to him three days before he died. I
bake my sister her favorite cookies, mail them to her with a poem.

We write our checks to the U.S. Treasury. My husband draws a
beautifully articulated hand with its middle finger raised in the
memo line.

My nephew turns 30 and I wonder how I got to be this old.

My hygienist tells me I have a geographic tongue, smooth island
patches that migrate across the surface, creating borders that shift,
a continental drift, a Pangaea in my mouth. *Don't be alarmed when
you look at it, it's harmless, it may be difficult to be reassured that
there is, in fact, nothing seriously wrong.*

I attend a funeral for someone I have never met. There is poetry,
good cake and punch that has definitely been spiked.

A truck cuts me off on the highway, with mud flaps that hold the
silhouettes of naked women and a bumper sticker that says,
assimilate or go back to your own country. For two days I cry for
no reason.

My friend's mother is in a coma. She holds her hand and hopes that
love is palpable through limp fingers, believes there is someone
who hears prayers for a living.

24

There are 357 structurally deficient bridges in my town and I've thought about driving off of every one of them.

I attend a friend's wedding and there is poetry and drunken toasts and possibility.

The maid of honor tells me her first job was taking calls for Ms. Cleo the psychic. *I became good at convincing people that disappointment is a sign they are moving closer to truth.*

I tell my doctor I have noticed a lump, it moves around my body, I feel sluggish and sometimes it's hard to breathe. He talks to me about the books he is reading and I feel better that he knows me enough to know that is what I need to hear now.

In the elementary school on the corner they install metal detectors. The phlebotomist who draws my blood has a shaved head and a neck tattoo. He is teenage girl thin and I tell him he is good at his job. I look at the wall and feel nothing as he fills vial after vial. He tells me, *I sell my plasma to make rent.*

The sound of my neighbor dumping a week's worth of wine bottles into the recycling bin is my new alarm every Monday.

At the airport I wait for my mom to return home after visiting my sister up north where it is still blowing snow in spring. I need to see her walk toward me, weary and smiling. As that tin can skids down the runway and bumps to a stop, I cry over the miracle of flight.

Here the trees are heavy with blooms, the sidewalks green with pollen. I slip on fallen gumballs from the tree I have been meaning to cut for years, eat Dayquil for breakfast.

Thousands of students walk out of schools, wear orange, raise signs, read poems.

When we are dead, all our clavicles and mandibles cracking, our perfect sets of ribs hugging us, all of our cavities equal, all calcium and cartilage—*see when we are skeletons how we were all identical, all along.*

Hydrangeas

are our wedding month. At first bloom, I scavenged
them in waves from all the best blooming spots—
the abandoned church on Llewellyn, the backyard bushes planted
by your grandmother, and from the corner building where 5 streets
meet amidst fast food and exhaust fumes, I hopped from the car
at a perfectly timed red light, ran between intersections
to harvest the overflowing bushes, their blue a beacon of calm.
Later, I wrap their stems in silk ribbons, carry them
down the aisle towards you, where you had always been.

You Are Not Honey, I Am Not Sugar (or why must all terms of endearment be sweet?)

Dearest, you are the bubbling yeast
at the top of the whiskey barrel
the brewing mash, warm and churning
spinning in the same rotation as the earth.
That vat is alive and you are the heat
a foaming Jacuzzi of chemistry.

You are a Picholine olive
the salt and brine I need
in the summer, a ripe
pamplemousse bursting,
a sprinkle of salt
on July watermelon.

You are baking powder, the lift,
the rise, the reaction. My love
you are crisp as a half-sour pickle,
every pregnant craving.

An artichoke peeled so, so slow—

leafy spikes discarded to reveal
the tender, toothy heart.

Kept Very Well

A peddler
and girl
pink as gum
a gourd-like
a horse
or a glue
factory
the bargain
had lost
its legs
not a day
an hour
gone by
he tried
to make money
easy enough
the real trap
that puzzling
feeling
was love

Cutting Teeth (Sticks and Stones)

He collects shark teeth, jagged and weathered,
memorizes and charts animal jaw strength
and clamps his tiny mouth into a donut, sugar
dusting his chin like pollen. When I tuck him
in, he will smell like sweat, grass and cinnamon.

He already knows how savage mouths are, tearing
holes in one another to ease their own pain. The bite
force of a lion rivals the strike of a crocodile. Biting
my tongue is worth a mouthful of blood, these days.

One in every thousand babies are born with teeth, his
mouth was never harmless. He worries his loose incisor
with his tongue, rocks it from his gum until it dangles.
My odd boy out who breaks so easy, smiles his black out grin.

Like playground fists, but passed notes, spit whispers
and taught taunts are like split lips to him, tender
neck peeks out from shell, each mock cracks him more.
As a girl, mom warned me to never pick on a turtle

If a snapper latches onto you, it won't let go 'til sundown.
Before bed he sorts his treasures. Tells me, *if you sever
a snake's head, it can still bite.* The wide triangles
of white sharks, the short blades of tiger sharks, the tapered
serrations of the nurse, his smile is a crossword puzzle
we solve together. At night we hum our lullaby,

but words will never harm me.

An Enigma in Pie

On the first day of summer
the owls fly out of the barn
we are at the kitchen counter learning
what not to do with piecrust
it's what you were taught from your aunts
when they decided it was time you found yourself a man
you seem to imply the same telling me to chill the butter
cut and slice it into flour, salt, and sugar; form little peas of dough
cross one hand over another sprinkling ice water like a blessing
you should bake with love—never make a pie crust when angry
it'll always come out tough, the less you work it, the more you
can make light, flaky, melt in your mouth marriage material
find someone you can feed—one hungry, holy mouth
what else is there but this moment hot and golden
this taste June sweat, firefly dance, ripe
from your own garden hands
sour rhubarb we've made sweet
this first bite, this who created this, who?

Honeysuckle

and the smell of mint is the overgrown garden I grew up with. It is the summer freedom of bike rides, cartwheels and days as long as my noon shadow. The fragrance was the night breeze from my open window, it was a stop on the rural road, reaching high up the vines of the ditch trees to pluck the buds, pinching the calyx and sliding it out of the petal, catching the liquid candy drop on my tongue, one after the other, guilty of stealing from the bees, dizzy with the scent and the buggy hum, knees weak from the men who hollered out their truck windows, hey girl, you're growing up fine, come see me tonight.

ripe

don't look up when it's peach
season there are dangers in the dropping
of ripened fruit heavy on limbs
new saplings struggle with their burden

train your eyes on the ground
to avoid bruised foreheads, a bloody nose
falling fruit is weaponry

the children of the pickers fill the bottoms
of their too big shirts, scooping
an arsenal of fruit from the ground to lob over
the rows at one another, flying
falling fruit a satisfying plop the squirt of overripe
peach flesh the honeyed sunset pulp
the fuzz so reminiscent of your teenaged face caught
between boy and man this skin like suede

if the sky gifts you a peach you may be drunk on summer
beware of pits those stones crack teeth

Hope without Light

You don't think of the dark in which
she was taken as swift and quiet as a fox

amongst the chickens. In the Cave of Swallows
in Mexico, the dark is so complete you can't see your hand

in front of your face, even though you know it exists
after all, is there attached to your arm

which aches from the weight of the child
you carried for days, shifting her from hip

to back, her wrists ragdoll limp around your neck,
her hip bones arrows in your ribs. You carried

her against you even as she diminished in the heat
so small it seemed she could be inside you again.

At night you do not think of the depression dark
blackness where even light from the stars can't reach

stars you know to be in the sky, know like faith, by heart:
the hunter and the bears, the fish who leaped forward

with each of your steps. In this asylum, you think only
of the birds each morning exiting the cave in their circles

flying upward, the swallows and the swifts sharing the same
center, spinning like the mixer paddles when you made

crème caramel in your small kitchen, beat the meringues
until they rose, in soft stiff peaks and the sound of so many

wings flapping towards light—The rush of all those feathers
moving the air over you in waves—At night they circle

the mouth of the cave and in groups that swirl like ink
they spin off and head straight down. When they cross

the edge, the birds tuck in their wings and free-fall, pulling
out of the dive when they reach the heights of their nests

such trust in the plunge, in knowing a nest will always be
home. She can no longer close her eyes when she prays—

must look for her daughter in every face that passes,
thinks she can still feel her hot breath at her ear.

Roses

That you fail to tend each year,
thrived without care.
You used to cut a single
rose and leave it in a plastic water bottle
on my desk before work each day—
in that heady summer
in that giddy dance of possibility.
When the fig tree filled in and the sticky mash
of ripened fruit squished between our toes

you called out the names of the roses like a chant:
Alchymist and Don Juan, the Duke of Edinburgh
and Gypsy Sue, the smell as cloying as a first kiss
back before I started pruning and fertilizing
researching soil acidity and cataloging hybrids

back before we felt thorns, before we grew
callouses—out our bedroom window the roses
languish on the shrub, cliché now, anyway.

Recoil

The corn had not been cut before the dove season
so temperate was the summer
my heart got caught doing something
right.
Early morning crack dawn clatters open
feathers spin to earth in lazy circles
spilling shots from shadows
shoulder hurt from the kick
blood on the tattered white.
Corn shaking their bent heads
no.
The wind found me
on my knees in supplication
cheek wet with dew
with doubt.

Visitation

Summers were mayonnaise
sandwiches warming in the sun
saltine crackers with a square
of neon orange cheese melted
in the microwave and topped
with a green olive plucked
from a martini glass—
pimento winking with gin
still strong pooling
in an oil slick of Velveeta
our cereal bobbed amongst lumps
of powdered milk that clung
to our tongues like Velcro—
fried bologna curled into a bowl
wobbled and popped in the pan
our hungry mouths open
and us always on the edge
of broke

Primroses

She grows the evening kind.
Delicate yellow petals bloom at night
under cover of dusk; the shy wallflowers
unfold.

My grandmother kept me tucked away
those long dog days. We'd creep outside
at twilight to watch the petals open, voyeurs
to this intimate undressing.

Green slowly unfolding, bending back
and yawning their petals left and right,
they wait for the night.
Just waking, releasing brilliance
from their shells.

In the gray evening, standing next
to her, we are eye to eye in bare feet,
and for magical minutes of stillness
like time-lapse photography the buds quiver;
so alive they breathe.

We would count them nightly to see
if there would be more than the one
summer after the heavy rains. Not wanting
to miss any late bloomers and their one chance to shine.

Because they die at first morning's light
as sun's rays wither the beauty.
We sneak out again at dawn to see
the startling show of yellow give one last
bow of lovely. The primrose in all properness
turns a deep peach color—

Like her red hair never graying just more
pale than the last visit—

before it shrivels, drops off the plant,
returns to the earth.

Cherries

As the blood that didn't appear
last month like the words we don't say
tears that fall thick as pits when blood spills
ache deep where a heartbeat cramped
in this galley you hold a stem between your teeth
beckon me come

What do I know of loss?

This is a new kind of quiet
the chickens squawk and peck,
the soft tuft of their heads bowing
over and over in prayer
the donkey brays and it is rusty
bedsprings, worn floorboards,
the creak of a tired porch swing
he wags his ears
looks at me with pity.

The bees make their own music
the farm cat kneads the dusty grass,
leaves exhale from their branch.
On my first walk down the road,
a possum is flattened on the gravel—
the crows circle and the flies feast
and something ate two chickens
last night, when we find their polished
bones, I cry

too soft for country life
if we cried over every dead thing
we would never survive out here.

Sunflowers

Don't mind humidity heavy

as a wool coat they don't mind

neglect and drought and the relentless
mid-day heat, they will find the sun as they

grow turning their head toward the light.
By the time they are mature they all
face east. The first time I saw them

I held my father's hand. They grew
near the cornfield and towered over me
while the monarchs flitted between the leaves
and dragonflies performed their dizzying dance
a ballet of flight and buzzing.

Every summer my height
was marked by those stalks, their sturdy stems
the bristles like my father's cheek. I was told
in this field faith and science meet
I traced patterns in that flower's face, brown
as my freckled shoulders, found the Fibonacci sequence
the looping arcs and saw their echo in the flowering
of artichokes, the uncurling fern of a pine cone,

the honeybee family tree, the spiraling seeds on a sunflower,
God's hand or the mysteries of math? I grew with them and still
they loomed, always there and taller than me, strong and sturdy.
When I saw the first one turn and wither its head slumping
like his face after dinner drinks, I cried to see it black and brittle.

Dad pointed at the sparrows circling
dipping in and out of those drooping
heads; the seeds were ready to harvest still giving all they had.
In a few days the whole patch was charred as grill ash.
Look close, you will find the fighter; one golden face
struggling to catch the light when all the rest have gone.
I place bouquets on his grave and pray that we may all come back
as birds in this buffet of sunflowers.

Terminal

In our last visit before hospice
made your bed in the living
room you sat up in your California
King, propped high
on pillows so fluffed they made
your diminishing form even smaller
you refused saltines, pushing the shiny
plastic sleeve away, and asked for toast.

Water drips from the faucet you will never fix.
In the garden, dust mingles with soil, rich
in compost and coffee grounds. As a child
I knelt to listen to the caterpillars
crawl on the tomatoes, the intermittent pop
of the bug zapper on the porch.
I could eat a whole loaf of bread then,
one hot, perfect, slice at a time thick with butter
that you slathered on my toast.

Outside a car alarm has been going off forever.
Every neighborhood dog is barking
I want to put us all out of our misery
but we are silent in this hot room.
What is the sound of organs shutting down?
The smell of neglected gums, the outrageous
length of an uncut toenail? The vacuum
hums and runs over the crumbs I've dropped
from the toaster, crisscrossing the same rug
in a pattern of stars, the bread and tracked in leaves
long gone the skin we've shed the fallen strips
of my tissue shreds tucked up my sweater sleeves

dust to dust earth to earth the soil—
all of this while buttering your toast
you take one bite declare it the best thing
you have tasted, these long sick months

Last Meal Requests of Texas Death Row Inmates 1932-2010

During the short but awful interval between sentence and execution, the prisoner shall be kept alone, and sustained with only bread and water.
—Blackstone's commentaries on the Laws of England.

Celery, cherries and a slice of cake.

Kentucky Fried Chicken and sugar-free black walnut ice cream.

A pound of strawberries.

Chicken Parmesan with Alfredo pasta.

Two pints of mint chocolate-chip ice cream.

A bag of Cheez Doodles and a can of Coca-Cola.

Assorted bag of Jolly Rancher candies.

A lump of dirt, a cup of yogurt.

Three Burger King Whoppers and a package of grape Hubba Bubba

A banana, a peach, a salad with ranch.

A single olive with the stone still in it.

Sea Currency

In the future when we are underwater
we will swim from pier to pier
rest our tired arms, catch our breath

we will still try to consume, even after losing
all our goods to flood, still try to control
the height of the tides, the pull of the moon.

Currency is shells and sea glass
we will barter with sea life,
dress in kelp, weave our hair with jellyfish

luminous at night they guide us deeper
into the lightness of salt, the freedom
of dark, finally weightless.

Starfish buy lightning, crabs make rain
the wisest and oldest—the lobsters and turtles
gather the hurricane winds when it's time to clear

us all again, we will forget what it feels like
to be dry, our skin pickled and puckered pink
sloughing off in shreds, where our scales form.

Colored buoys hang on driftwood
like a mobile from the clouds
some days we see our former lives bobbing along—

all the waterlogged accent pillows, the shoes, (such
restrictive things), coffee mugs and cologne bottles
that we tuck our notes into, rolled on cigarette papers

written with squid ink, we try to hold onto the last things
we remember, how the pillow remembers the head,
how the mirror looks for its daily visitors

after the storms churn us in circles
we are part of each other's orbit now,
knowing the flip of a fin turns ripples into waves.

We know that the shark must eat
and the tuna must eat
and the mollusk must eat

and this is where we are
at the bottom of the chain, bellies
scraping coral, siphoning sand, filtering
krill until we are finally happy
with what we have

and forget that we were ever alone.

Making Progress

My ancestors bred sheep, death
and cobwebs, twisters, the rolling waves
of storm clouds on the horizon

plump and slow in a two-piece suit
I stroll unaware towards a Genie I've unlocked
you can't listen to the core of your need when you speak

worry, sweet and sharp as bamboo sticks
I wish for one more tango, a silk dress, the curve of my foot in a
stiletto
these days I am robes and baggage that doesn't travel

eclipsing the earth and dreaming of the underbelly of salmon
buttery and pink as tongue, the pillow of a perfectly crimped
dumpling, the rising steam of broth

sweet honey drip of bourbon hot
salt like comet trails a study in rarities
like honeybees 20 years from now

the carpenter ants will still march forward determined
and strong together, as I watch anchored by time that unreels like
light

Crape Myrtle

When all other
flowers are exhausted
from the heat,
the blooms burst
from the trees
umbrellas of pink
and purple petals
hang in clumps
of confetti stippling
streets, a fiesta
of late summer
this blaze into
autumn, a glorious
show, the lead
role for late
bloomers quenches our
parched August mouths
firebird, pink lace
petite embers, snow

Shedding bark in
strips like sunburned
skin peeling pale
gray as mice
means it's time
for pruning this
practice of crape
murder, lopped off
branches from the
trunk shorn and
jagged limbs akimbo
we take the branches
turned upside down
they become walking

stick insects parading
high knees kicking
through the flowered
grass like stilt-walkers.

These southern streets
could be Cleveland
if it weren't
for these trees

Brood

Quiet like honey dripping
off your spoon into the morning tea
was how they first arrived that summer
after the second cancer diagnosis, it seemed
like nothing at first, a hum, so little had changed
but then the whirring began, as they broke ground
and rose into a cloud, first at night as you tried to find
the cool place on your pillow, out the window in the giant
oak, the alpha brood of cicadas buzzed and grew into a symphony
all night and all day as the drugs slowly dripped into your veins
was the sound of their chorus growing, their wings rubbing, their
love breeding tymbal drum of urges, the droning high pitched alien
pulse strumming the air a pulse that kept you numb. You were

obsessed each time we talked, you had
learned more of their story, their habits, swarm
cycles, their underground life spans, their so short
summers and you studied the rise and fall of their song
like it was your own breath, like it was the beat of your own
heart keeping you here another day. Always the nagging mind
that this would be your last witness, your last opportunity as
biographer of this species in their glory, their hot whiskey summer
bliss. Their cryptic night song kept you up and you dozed in the
day, dreamt your arms had become wings, that your stomach was
shell, that you bedded between leaves, fed on sap and laid eggs in
the slit of the tree bark, an underground nymph waiting for her
moment to rise, to fly, to reproduce. After all that soil dark
and cool, the sun is astonishing how it shone through your
outstretched limbs, heart open as a hymnal when they
began dropping like fat pinecones to the ground, their
husks littered the lawn by the shovelful and you

read they were edible, *shrimp of the land* and
the thought turned my stomach yet
you wondered at their taste, what
if you had a craving

and they were gone, you harvested them in your palm
early morning, blanched them like lobster, dunked
in ice water, and after you separated the wings
and the legs, you closed your eyes and bit
the flesh, the earth

quiet like the hollow still clinging to the bark of a tree.

Crossing

The moon is a peach slice in the summer sky
cut by a paring knife held in God's hand.
I walk towards you barefoot through the grass
in the wet morning of weaving spiders
as you lead me by the hand.

We left the cabin still and sleeping
snuck to the lake daring each other. You stole
the canoe, I sank in the water, took a breath and swam.
With every inhalation I saw you paddling beside me
across that long, silent lake to the hot springs a mile away.

In the deepest center of the lake, the cold shock
the pure dark draw, I stall
with thoughts of sliding under
            the nothing but water and moonglow

When there is nothing but dark
thoughts of sliding under
I hear the sound of the oar,
your smooth motion matching
the rhythm of my stroke.

You are there with each breath
guiding me. God is in the details,
in the spray of stars that outnumber prayers.

Breathe with me now, like you did
so I can remember what it's like to break
the surface.

Naming

My mother-in-law would not waste
a fruit, even fallen from a plant,
bruised or bitten, it would hurt
her to swat the aphid munching
the tomatoes or to not carry
a spider in the palm of her hand
out of the house to the earth

her garden is somewhere
between jungle and Eden
she keeps bees and harvests
milkweed for the monarchs,
raising them from caterpillar
through chrysalis, tagging
and tracking them on their
flight south. She believes
in flying things, named
her only son, Adam—
because it was he
who named the birds.

on the day she decides to leave

she eats a modest breakfast alongside
her husband of 20 years, happy
to have cooked him the ham he
likes even though she rarely keeps
it in the house anymore
she works in the garden pruning
the late-blooming tomatoes, weeding—
the work that is never done

she goes inside for a nap, she says, too much
sun, a headache—
kisses her spouse on his rough cheek,
pats the head of the dog
that sweet tuft behind the ears
closes the bedroom door swallows
the handful of pills stretches out
with her pen and notepad careful
of her cursive, each word curling
towards the ends until the letters
trail off with her slumped hand

on the day she decides to leave us
we come over to visit instead
of waiting until next week
like planned and in the moment
after the doorbell stopped chiming
through the house our voices
reaching up the stairs, she dumps
her cupped hand of blue pain
pills into the toilet and flushes

on the day she decides she'll die
the paramedics do not slow down
for a dog loose in the street
for a pedestrian stumbling
in the intersection for cars that
ignored the sirens, they arrive
just minutes after the call when
they can still work their movie
medical miracles of paddles
and clear and the *beep beep*
beep of a heart

on the day she decides
not to get up to lay in bed
a little longer to try to decipher
which songbird sits on the branch
by the window she reaches
for her partner who says

let's leave for the day let's
drive until we run out of road until
we see something new, until
we remember how to talk
with each other until
we are dizzy with life

let the tomatoes rot on the vine
and the weeds grow wild

Drowning

How long is the longest breath
you can hold? How long the grudge

of silence? How do you fight buoyancy
so well? Swelling your lungs with birdshot—

The slow rain bends the stems
of the tall weeds like piano keys.

In the steeple of your hands we lean in again

of the tall weeds like piano keys
the slow rain bends the stems

so well swelling your lungs with birdshot
of silence, how do you fight buoyancy?

You can hold, how long the grudge,
how long is the longest breath?

Chrysanthemums

The sun knocked the wind out of us when the night fell so fast
we knew fall was here with every reddened leaf, every leaving
bird flying south, the streetlights flicked to life before dinner.
The mums appeared burning gold and orange in their patio pots
that fall it seemed all the fathers had to fly away to war
yellow ribbons hung above chrysanthemums from every stoop on
the street.

Everything has to die, he said when we turned over the stiff rabbit
from the raked pile of jumping leaves, its fur still soft as mittens.
The flower petals like embers all seemed poised to wave goodbye.

A Recipe for Remembering

One unpronounceable diagnosis
three dozen squirreled away Percocet
a rich batter
a preheated late summer afternoon
a tight bundle of cut sticks
a table full of end-season tomatoes
bursting and split at their stems
lazy fruit flies full and dizzy drunk
hover thick near the light
a cracked egg gone cold in the skillet
rubber edged and leaking yolk
there is not enough tension tamer
tea in the world—the kettle screams
incessant mix
together a birthday, the anniversaries
boat fuel and firearm solvent
the vibrations of a clam rake
a smile welcome
as the flowers in May

stir together breath
and not breath, blood
and sinew, tissues wrung
dry between worried
fingers, two cups of tears
have they ever stopped?
do not add salt
the same words again
the same
words again the
same words
fold again, sift, knead

bake at 1600 degrees
the temperature at which
a body is ashes
in a simple box
tidy and square
a breadbox to remember
a loaf to leave, a leavening
an offering.

Lack

Salt splits the sidewalks in cracks,
throws up chunks of concrete like loose
bricks, far more treacherous than the ice
it was meant to melt. In Northern towns
the roads wear the scars of salt.

Wars waged over this, empires gained
or lost, white grains found on altars
in pages of holy books, purity used
in exchange for slaves. The ones not worth
their salt were tossed.

Traded for silks, cumin, and people—
pork, beef, and fat, it preserves, cures and wounds.
Mourning tastes like salt, that ocean that never sates thirst.
Salt curing mummies aided the soul into the afterlife.
Pinched, thrown over the shoulder for luck,
or to ward off the Devil.

In the heart of February, far from home, I trace
ice patterns like the corners of my grandmother's eyes,
her people salt of the earth. Stepping slowly, I can't stop
thinking of Napoleon's troops marching in the cold retreat
from Moscow. How they died on snowdrifts, their wounds
unable to heal for lack of salt.

How I Got a Kitten

The first time was six weeks
after a hasty marriage: still a teen,
a mistake, I knew; immediately
after *I do*. Read the instructions
three times and sat in the cramped
apartment bathroom praying
for that thin pink negative

which came on a wave of relief
that would become so familiar.

The next time near the end of that
mess, a last desperate attempt
at a family, pacing the hallway
of my sister's house and begging
some patron saint of tests for
a slim line that severs my ties
to this man cleanly, of course

it comes as inevitably
as salmon spawn upstream.

The third time it was all wrong—
rebound, drugstore bathroom,
regret and worry like a noisy
thief, the seconds pass in sync
with the dripping sink, mold
climbs the corner tiles, angry
at everything, a lost puzzle piece.

There it is, single pink minus
just mine, not us, old friend.

Another aisle, the right vows,
the death do us part love, when
test results 4 through 9 come in
waves that range from adamant belief
that this is the last thing we want,
to an uncertain maybe, to a hope
#babymakesthree

10 was loss and loss and loss
the confirmation of impossible.

Today my love comes home
with a kitten, pink and mewing.

At night it kneads my stomach
falls asleep on my pillow,

I try not to hate it.

Saucier

It's Valentines and though we have passed
these last weeks between hot tempers
and clenched teeth, I am making your favorite
a time consuming layered dish—
Greek Moussaka, we shared it once in a postcard
as we sat on the water's edge in Mykonos,
a cat at our feet, the wind blowing our hair

Here I am stirring béchamel slowly, focusing
on the careful addition of the cream
to the buttery roux, one of the mother sauces
of French cuisine—sauce that completes a thing—
in another life I could have been
a saucier in the kitchen brigade
a whisk an extension of my hand

stirring becomes a trance until
the sauce is luxurious
and slides off the back of the spoon
like my silk wedding slip
as you brushed it from my shoulders
to a pool on the wood floor of our first home

you pull me from the stove, hum *Summer Wind*
kiss the garlic on my fingers, it is hard
to say whether the birds squawking
on our lawn are fighting or mating—
sometimes there is no difference.

What Do You See?

I see the rain,
you see a shallow
puddle with a moon reflected
a birdbath catfight
the sprout of a birch tree
we could quibble over colors
pick each other slick as the inside
of an oyster or shined as a cockleshell
the tinfoil crown of dress up
the queen of hazard
the dazzle of fever
if I could ink a tattoo of you
that would bellow love
through these veins
humor you with an etching
on my skin as extra as Velcro
over shoelaces, I would paint
your head in profile
the way it looks each morning
when you kiss me goodbye
I will say *gray* you will say *silver*
either way our hair lays curled
on our paired pillows soft as shadow
each gray hair I pluck from my head
you call silver, shining like tinsel
I see an unraveled winter wool thread
stubborn as stiff collars
I see age and you see our life
together this love of years
as fine as hairs
splitting, turning sterling night
after glowing night

Holly

In the snow our world was made
quiet, it softened every word and blurred
the bruises into blooms, made everything
so blindingly clean and white; it hurt to look
too long at sun glowing on snowdrifts
we made forts and tunnels, packed them hard
like igloos and ate snowcream by the fistful, we stayed
outside until our toes and fingers stung numb
like split lips, we were wild.

Inside, the ice made lacey patterns on the windows
and the tree branches seemed to shiver in their crystal coats
you hated the indoors, would tolerate it just enough
gain feeling in your limbs, sip some soup and head back out
to be a Siberian explorer, a polar bear, an astronaut—anyone
but the boy who couldn't sleep at night scared of hands that
appeared under covers, the one who'd later be found behind
the shed dead from a .22 to the head, blood bright as holly
berries scattered on the snow.

Carnivore

After I left you, I left meat for years
all those briskets, pork loins, cracked

racks of ribs, shanks and lamb crowns
with their shiny tips, ivory tusks spearing

the air between us at silent dinners
all the grilling and roasting, the braising

and basting, the perfect overnight marinades.
In the meat years, I dreamt I was thin enough

that bones stuck out from my skin like white
banners of surrender. You liked exposing

them, each French cut long boned rib-eye.
You often said I had too much meat

on my bones, still you fed me all those roasted
animals after I had spent most of this life eating

from a garden, practicing non-harm.
If you are dreaming of bones, in real life

you should be wary of treachery
and hypocrites; a fighting spirit

is what is needed, but I was weak
and you were an artist with a boning

knife, cleaning away the fat and sinew
trimming as close to bare as possible

carving me into something
I hardly recognized.

Butchery is complicated and contains cuts
made up in different shops across

the country, men who work to get
the most from a piece of meat, animals

don't come marked with maps of slice
lines to separate the filet mignon
from the tenderloin. They invented
cuts, the country-style ribs, meat with

nothing to cling to but shoulder blade
or the tri-tip, the sirloin muscle 50's

housewives bought as roast, stretching
their thin budgets and warming stomachs.

You sized up every side of beef
you saw, rated the marbling and called

it a prime cut. You loved osso buco
and the thought of those calves in tiny

pens in the dark, hurt my heart.
You said that no one could ever love me

the way that you do. I dreamt
with my eyes open, seeing bones

in dreams means there is work to be done
If you dream of fish bones, see the perfect

lacy outline of each brittle fin, then
you are full of regret. To dream of a whole

skeleton is a sign you should reconsider
the structure of your life, so I left

you, the meat, the bones, the taste of blood
in my mouth. I was so very hungry.

Bones

In anthropology class my professor held
up a photo of *man's first calendar,* a bone

with 28 incisions carved in it. What man
needs to record 28 days? This would be

woman's first calendar. She saved the cleaned
parched bone from the stewpot, noting the size

of the moon how it moved from fingernail
to grinning fool, and marked each change

with a sharpened stone, her own change
from tender belly bloat and blood

moon to new moon, the wax and wane
a baby tied tight to the hip, scratching

out the days to prevent the next swelling.
It was she who kept them fed, carved

the meat from the bones after the hunt
worked slowly and reverently to honor

the stilled breath, the glazed eyes, the chest
gone cold, using every part of the deer

to sustain them until the berries grew
from the leaves. The lungs boiled, liver

grilled, the kidneys for the babies, with
each cut she made she hummed a windsong

and secretly sliced the heart
into moon shaped slivers just

for her to eat in the dark
where only she could see it glow.

Even now I still smell
blood on my hands.

Prosperity

Our friend who is like family has become an international mystery: she and her diplomat husband now in Kuala Lumpur soon to be in Shanghai has come from Heathrow two days in the states for a wedding, meets us for lunch on the boardwalk, kisses on both cheeks wishes a happy lunar new year.

Tells of her youngest who was all mermaids and dress up when they left us, is near fluent in Chinese, scuba dives in Bali, has met Jane Goodall and can discuss the intricacies of Vietnamese cuisine. We order our diner food, try to keep up with the rapid-fire stories of her Malay New Year's adventure.

Yee Sang, a raw fish salad, a riot of colors; candied orange peel, red radish strips, curling ribbons of carrot, sliced ginger, green onion, crushed peanuts and pomelo, around salmon sliced so thin you can see through it, everything rosy and soft.

Tradition is for each diner to work together as ingredients are added—tossed into the air with a loud declaration of wishes, the height of the toss reflects the height of fortunes.
"Prosperous wishes" *jíxiáng huà* is what is said with each toss, loudly enthusiastically. A newly transplanted American man joined them, fresh to the consulate and clumsy with chopsticks.

In Chinese the word for fish is very similar to surplus, abundance, vigor. In Chinese the word for wish, pronounced with a foreign tongue, and a stress on the high syllable is the vulgar slang for the male anatomy.

"Prosperous cocks," he shouts and tosses, "prosperous cocks!" The Malay women blush. No one corrects him.

She laughs and orders tomato soup, says she can't get anything near it in Asia.

We eat our dry tuna melts, say we haven't been up to much.

Superbloom

After ten years of parched winters, the desert
has revealed what it contained all along
the colors are vivid as a praise song
sprawling wildflowers where there was dirt
wrapped snug in wax coats the seeds lie dormant
on barren ground for years, washed and softened
as rains came they cracked open and beckoned
roots to push through rocky earth, this ancient

dance of sun's warmth and gentle winds they bloom
complete their life cycle, poppies, gold brush,
lupine and baby blues, a color boom
from space, a patchwork quilt, a carpet lush
feast for bees, rain brought the drought to its knees
they tried to bury us, but we were seeds.

A Baker's Dozen—Ways of Looking at a Woman

Cup size and the circumference
of her thighs, measurements and numbers,
weight as mass within a given gravity field

Mr. So and So's daughter,
Mr. So and So's wife,
Mr. So and So's widow

Apples and pears, a new kind
of edible fruit bouquet. All flesh
and juice, all digestible

Soft and frightened as a fawn
pink as candy floss
sweet and cheap as a carnival prize

Labor on the fields, labor in the kitchen
on her back, on her knees
bearing, bearing, bearing

A vessel, moist and dark
a trophy, a notch, a lay
belted, latched, shamed, silenced

Mistress of brews and chants
grower, sower, cultivator, forager she
who makes something with nothing

Gossip and talk all mouth
and tongue, tart, loose
lipped liar, what she asked for

Nymph, siren, oracle, she of four arms
eyes in the back of her head, webspinner
spit that cures, that combs, that cleans

Bound foot, lotus, calloused foot, leather
feet washed and oiled, petals sprinkled
in her steps so light they do not leave a print

Food for the wolf, fuel for the fire
damsel, dumbstruck, jealous cat
her place is her place is her place

Torchbearer, bra-burner, riveter
warrior, protector, gossamer moth of light
she who picks up all the pieces

A person in her own right
the half-life of a halo glowing gold
with fire: lightning igniting

About the Author

Kindra McDonald received her MFA from Queens University of Charlotte. She teaches poetry classes at The Muse Writers Center in Norfolk, VA and is an adjunct writing professor and sometimes doctoral student. Her work has appeared in various journals and anthologies. She has been nominated for a Pushcart Prize and Bettering American Poetry. She is the author of the chapbooks *Concealed Weapons* and *Elements and Briars*. Her poetry book *Fossils* was published by Finishing Line Press in 2019. She lives with her husband in the city of mermaids where she wrangles cats, bakes cakes, hikes and makes mixed-media art.